Eucharistic Consecration

Colin Buchanan

Bishop of Woolwich

GROVE BOOKS LIMITED
RIDLEY HALL RD CAMBRIDGE CB3 9HU

Contents

Foreword

I am writing this booklet at the point where both eucharistic liturgy in general, and eucharistic prayers in particular, are up for re-thinking and re-writing in the Church of England. As those texts are in a fluid state, this short booklet cannot deal with them in detail. However, I have been encouraged by the Group for Renewal of Worship (GROW), the group of authors which I chair, to think there may be a place at this stage in the re-thinking for a general treatment of broad points of both interest and controversy. I owe a special debt to Chris Cocksworth and Trevor Lloyd for reading and evaluating the material in draft. I should add that I am aware of the apparently controversial character of the case I put forward, and, whilst I believe in robust combat, even in theology, I would not willingly give gratuitous hurt to people from whom I differ. I only ask that readers should try to see it, at least while reading it, the way I have encountered and understood the issues.

The Cover Illustration is by the Benedictine Nuns of Turvey Abbey
© McCrimmon Publishing Co Ltd. Used with permission.

First Impression August 1998
ISSN 0144-1728
ISBN 1 85174 381 2

1
Outlining the Problems

The Lord Jesus, in the night in which he was betrayed, took bread, and when he had given thanks he broke it and said 'This is my body which is for you. Do this in commemoration of me.'

1 Corinthians 11.23–24

Gregory Dix wrote of those last few words 'Was ever command so obeyed?' But we might equally ask of the previous words ('This is my body'): 'Was ever a statement so debated?' It is a debate which has roots in the apostolic church and the discourse in John 6, presumably written up in the 90s AD,[1] a debate which takes a different form in the time of Ignatius of Antioch,[2] a debate which may well be fuelled by the cryptic explanation of Justin Martyr in the mid-second century, a debate enormously exaggerated by medieval excesses, and thus a debate which bade fair to dominate the Reformation conflicts (which were surely actually rooted elsewhere?). It is a debate which has run on, for reasons to be noted, in the post-Reformation life of the Church of England (and of the other Provinces of the Anglican Communion). So no one writing a Grove booklet towards the end of the twentieth century can expect to conclude the debate with a smartly formulated rabbit out of a doctrinal hat.[3] Indeed any attempt to address the question closely is liable to cause offence rather than resolve conflict.

Nevertheless, the question is worth addressing. We have an immutable original scriptural text in 'This is my body.' Whilst there are variants in the different accounts in the synoptics and Paul (and the John 6 passage), there is no escaping the use by Jesus at that last supper of these basic texts: 'This is my body' and 'This is my blood.' No-one attempting to 'Do this' today can avoid the terminology; all must make something of it, give an explanation to newcomers, reach a resolution in their own hearts, and approach the table at peace with the terminology and ready to find positive nourishment in it.

---

1 It has been conventional for Roman Catholics to interpret John 6.66 ('From this time on many of his disciples went away and no longer walked with him') as a reaction against the robust sacramental language of verses 32–58—that is, the hearers could not cope with the cannibalistic terminology. If so, then the seeds of conflict are sown during Jesus' earthly ministry, as he deliberately stakes his gift of salvation upon this extraordinary language, and thus produces division among his disciples. It is, on this view, a division overtly arising from his choice of language, as, when Jesus asks the twelve whether they too will depart, Simon Peter replies 'Lord, to whom shall we go? You have *the words of eternal life*' (John 6.67–68). However, a latter day non-Roman may well take the view that there are other dividing-points raised by Jesus, not least in verses 61–65, which might more plausibly be held to have precipitated the departure of the many and the adherence of the twelve.
2 The Gnostics 'deny that the eucharist is the very flesh of Christ' (*Smyrnaeans* 6). What then were the orthodox supposed to assert?
3 I was tempted to write *Deus ex machina*, but forbore.

In brief the crucial points in debate are two.

Firstly, what does it mean to describe bread as Christ's body? What has 'happened' to bread to be thus characterized? Using slightly post-biblical language, we ask 'What has "consecration" done to the bread?'

Secondly, what conditions must be met to warrant our use of such a language? Going again to the language of consecration, we ask 'What action, language or ritual "consecrates" the bread to become the body of Christ?'

There are two totally different questions here; firstly, what does consecration effect? Secondly, what effects consecration? Whilst the two are deeply linked, and whilst answering one inevitably requires us to answer the other, they are distinct, they do admit of different combinations of answers, and, paradoxically, they do seem to require to be answered in the inverse order to that of strict chronology. The question 'What does consecration effect?' lies somewhere in the realm of sacramental theology and may lead to a metaphysical answer—or possibly a circular argument. The question 'What effects consecration?' lies in the field of liturgical theology and should lead to a liturgical answer.

This booklet tackles the two questions in that order.

2

What Does Consecration Effect?

Some Biblical Perspectives

Here then is the first question. What did Jesus *mean* when he said 'This is my body,' and how did he expect his followers to understand him? We may address the question by first of all inflating it to its most paradoxical formulation. Here then are some propositions:

1. Jesus not only said 'This is my body'; he also said 'Take, eat, this is my body.' So *eating his body* is central to the whole issue.
2. In John's gospel he said 'Unless you *scrunch the flesh* of the Son of Man and drink his blood, you have no life in you.' So the wording used is extremely physical.[4]
3. Paul wrote 'The bread which we break, is it not a sharing [or communion or participation or fellowship] in the body of Christ?'[5] The immediately preceding discussion says that, under the Jewish dispensation, those who ate the

---

4 The Greek verb '*trogo*' used in John 6 might be rendered 'scrunch' or 'munch,' and has at least some hints of the *mode* of ingestion and not merely the result.

5 The Greek word here—*koinonia*—can have any of these meanings in English.

sacrificed animals were 'sharers [*or* participants etc] in the altar'—and that those who eat of animals sacrificed to demons are at risk of being sharers with demons. So the 'sharing in the body of Christ' must be, by logic of the argument, *by eating*.

4. Paul also wrote that the worshipper should engage in self-examination and on that basis eat the bread and drink the cup, for there is, in the eating and drinking, a judgment one brings on oneself (1 Cor 11.28–29).

The issue posed by these propositions may mean we should restate the original question, for the central biblical question would now appear to be: what are the worshippers eating and drinking when they receive the bread and wine of the eucharist? It is a question which sits slightly uneasily with the static question: in what sense is the bread or the wine to be viewed and described as the body or the blood of the Lord? And yet, on further inspection, it would seem to be the question set by the original context of the Last Supper; if Jesus gave the bread to his disciples and said 'Take, eat; this is my body' (Matt 26.26; cf Mark 14.22, Luke 22.19), then it is arguable that the definitive words about the bread being his body are *words of distribution*, and not of some prior 'consecration.'

This kind of approach locates the vital action of the sacrament in the distribution, in the giving and receiving, of the bread and wine. The command is a command to 'take, eat' and the interpretative words ('This is my body') relate to bread which is being passed to the disciples as the Lord says them.

The Parallel with Baptism

Before we go on to look more closely at those interpretative words, it may be useful to note a parallelism here with baptism. The concept of two 'sacraments'— one of beginning, one of continuing—is not itself using scriptural terminology, but it is a construction upon scriptural evidence. In general, the idea of a sacrament has been accepted within historic Christianity, and from the Reformation onwards a sacrament has been defined in the Churches of the Reformation as 'an outward and visible sign of an inward and spiritual grace given to us ordained by Christ himself...'[6] On this reckoning, there are two sacraments, baptism and the eucharist, the 'ordaining' of which can be safely traced to the institution of Christ. And the point of this present discussion is that in baptism the outward part of the sacrament consists solely in the actual application or administration of the water to the candidate. There may be a prayer over the water in advance, but a baptism is still a baptism without that prayer (as is shown in the provisions for emergency baptism). Whatever is conveyed to the candidate in baptism is conveyed through the giving and receiving of the water, but is not 'in' the water. The parallel thinking would suggest that we look for the giving and receiving of the bread and wine of the eucharist to convey certain benefits (or possibly judgment), but would

---

6   The quotation is taken from the Catechism in the *Book of Common Prayer*, from the section on the sacraments which was added in 1604.

5

not expect to look for those benefits 'in' the bread and wine. The parallel with baptism was of great importance to the English Reformers, and is well expressed in the 'epiclesis' which Cranmer wrote into the 1552 communion service:

> '…and grant that *we, receiving* these thy creatures of bread and wine, in accordance with thy Son our Saviour Jesus Christ's holy institution, in remembrance of his death and passion, *may be partakers* of his most blessed body and blood.'

The italics are mine; the *locus* of the body and blood of Christ was to be in the *reception* of the bread and wine.

Post-biblical Developments

The logic of this radical Reformation re-writing of liturgy would seem to be in total accord with Scripture; but it ducks and omits a vast history of eucharistic developments in the intervening fifteen centuries, a history which bears upon us in many ways and must certainly be briefly visited if we are to understand the shape of questions to-day.

It is not difficult to trace the slow veering away from the New Testament emphasis, a slow changing over the generations such that no one generation would think they were different from their immediate predecessors. This slow changing happens with concepts of eucharistic sacrifice; it happens with the actual reception of communion; it happens with ceremonial; it happens with the 'votive' value put on the eucharist; it happens with the unplanned distancing of the Latin language from the language of the people, as the latter changes in Western Europe into Romance languages; and thus there appears over the centuries to be a wholesale drift away from the simplicity and straightness of Jesus' command to 'do this.' And the understanding of 'This is my body' was all part of the drift. No doubt this was partly because of the breadth of interpretation to which Jesus' words were open, if taken on their own; but it also seems to have involved a kind of spiritual auction, in which generations attempted to outstrip their predecessors in the higher and higher valuation they could place on the 'body' and 'blood' terminology. A few brief glimpses at passing history will establish the trend.

1. Ignatius of Antioch (c110 AD)

> '[The heretics] do not allow that the eucharist is the flesh of our Saviour Jesus Christ…' (*Smyrnaeans* 6)

2. Justin Martyr (c150 AD)

> '…as Jesus Christ our Saviour being made flesh through the word of God took both flesh and blood for our salvation, so also were we taught that the food for which thanks are given [*or* 'which is eucharisticized'] by the word of prayer which comes from him—food by which flesh and blood through conversion are nourished—is both the flesh and blood of that Jesus who was made flesh.' (*Apol* 1.66)

3. Ambrose (c380 AD)

'He [the bishop presiding at the eucharist] says, "who, the day before he suffered, took bread in his holy hands." Before it is consecrated, it is bread; but when the words of Christ are added, it is the body of Christ. Then hear his words: "Take...for this is my body." And before the words of Christ, the cup is full of wine and water; when the words of Christ have been employed, the blood is created which redeems his people...' (*De Sacramentis*, para 23)

4. From the Ninth to the Thirteenth Centuries

There are three significant watersheds in this period for our purposes. In the ninth century at the French monastery of Corbie there was a controversy between two monks. Paschasius wrote a monograph on the eucharist with a very strong 'realist' doctrine of localized presence—stating that the bread is the literal flesh of Christ, as risen from the dead and then multiplied on earth by a miracle. He was opposed by another monk, Ratram (or Bertram), who taught a symbolic view. This controversy is notable as probably the last point in Roman history when a genuine (level playing-field) debate was possible; or, to put it another way, it was the last point at which doctrine such as Ratram's would survive uncondemned (though it was, unsurprisingly, condemned two centuries later)...[7]

The second watershed came with Berengarius of Tours in the eleventh century. He taught a doctrine of a real presence of Christ, but without any material change occurring in the elements. He was almost universally opposed, and it is clear, from the vantage point of history, that he was the last to be able to question any of the growing consensus moving towards transubstantiation. He was not on anything like a level playing-field, but he was apparently able to avoid formal condemnation, perhaps because there was arguably still no defined official doctrine—for all that it was coming.

The last stage was the move to a defined statement. This was adumbrated by Peter Lombard in his *Sententiae* in the middle of the twelfth century, and was then promulgated as 'transubstantiation' at the Fourth Lateran Council (text below).

5. Fourth Lateran Council (1215)

'In this church also he himself, Jesus Christ, is priest and sacrifice; his body and blood are contained in the sacrament of the altar under the species of bread and wine; these are transubstantiated, the bread into the body, the wine into the blood, by divine power in order that, to complete the mystery of his union with us, we ourselves may receive from his person what he himself has received from ours.'[8]

---

7   It later played a contributory role in the thinking of the English Reformers, particularly Nicholas Ridley.
8   The original Latin of this extract from Canon I reads:
    'In qua [ecclesia] idem ipse sacerdos, et sacrificium Jesus Christus: cuius corpus et sanguis in sacramento altaris sub speciebus panis et vini veraciter continentur: transsubstantiatis, pane in corpus, et vino in sanguinem, potestate divina, ut ad perficiendum mysterium unitatis accipiamus ipsi de suo quod accepit ipse de nostro.'

This is the point at which the word 'transubstantiation' enters the historical discourse; and it is soon after defined by Aquinas in Aristotelian terms of 'substance' (which truly changes from being bread to being the body of Christ) and 'accidents' (which remain unchangingly those of bread). This happily chimed in with the universality in the West of the unleavened wafer, which had a sharp-edged outline, produced virtually no crumbs when broken, and could be kept (or reserved) for a good period of time.[9] The doctrine led, of course, to further abuses—a reinforcing of the doctrine of mass sacrifice, the withdrawal of the cup from the laity, the consequent delay in admitting baptized children to communion, a final shift in the general lay purpose in attending mass from receiving communion to adoring the elevated host, a consequent further gulf between clergy and laity (itself exacerbated by the almost invariable adoption of the 'Eastward' position of the priest), and the growth of extra-liturgical eucharistic devotions (including Corpus Christi processions, which began just fifty years after the Lateran Council).

At first sight, therefore, it may appear that the two opposed schools of interpretation of our Lord's words might also be distinguished by whether or not their respective distribution has a preceding 'consecration'—as (at first sight) a receptionist doctrine does not require such a portentous moment and a 'realist' or 'localized' one does.

It is not, however, quite so clear as that. In all schools of thought, there may well be a case for separating 'consecration' from distribution. It is obviously perfectly possible to designate or earmark particular stocks of bread and wine, in advance of the eating or drinking of them, as those which are to be used for this sacramental purpose; and that designation could appropriately be termed 'consecration.' In the process an actual *sequence* of events (dare one say a 'shape'?) then gives a clearer ground-plan to a liturgy. Such a shape and sequence to the meal enables the liturgical provision prior to the actual eating and drinking to be purposeful. On any analysis we are unlikely to be saying that the action of the Lord's Supper is so uniquely bound up in the distribution of the bread and wine that no prior warning need be available that this *is* the Lord's Supper. That would be absurd, and perhaps the 'prior warning'—the backdrop to the distribution—will inevitably give rise to notions of 'consecration.'[10] That in itself means that a careful enquiry into what is to be deemed to effect consecration must go closely with the issue of what consecration effects; and that separate enquiry follows in

9 The canonical requirement of the wafer went back to the 'azymes' (or 'unleavened') controversy preceding the Great Schism (and with origins in the ninth century), when, for biblical/ historical reasons, the church in the West claimed it was right to use unleavened bread—and the relationship of that wafer to the later doctrine of transubstantiation was one of sheer coincidence, in which the prior existence of the wafer provided both a credibility for the doctrine and a reasonably manageable programme of reverent usage.

10 Cranmer's 1552 rite, which so obviously and deliberately locates 'consecration' within the actual distribution and reception, nevertheless uses the narrative of institution as that backdrop and, from one point of view, thus invited later generations to make more of the narrative than Cranmer himself was doing. See my *What Did Cranmer Think He Was Doing?* (Grove Liturgical Study No 7, Grove Books, 1976).

chapter 3. For the moment, the establishing that in principle a process entitled 'consecration' can precede the distribution sets us on the search for what that in itself will effect, consonant with the language of Scripture.

The Meaning of 'This is My Body,' 'This is My Blood'

We have seen that the non-negotiable feature of any enquiry or discussion is that Jesus said 'This is my body' and 'This is my blood.' Any liturgical text which draws upon the institution of the rite by Jesus is bound to return to those words. No solution of awkward questions, or evasion of unwelcome answers, is available by simply eliminating the terminology—including the governing verbs 'Eat...my body' and 'Drink...my blood.' We have to keep the terminology and wrestle with its meaning. But it seems reasonable to start by saying that there is here either something of the most ghastly (though fantasy-ridden) cannibalism, or of an amazing God-given gift of enormous value. If we would keep our trust in our Lord, then we conclude that this is an amazing gift—but one which, however dangerous-sounding its terminology, cannot and must not be confused with cannibalism.

We have also seen that the determinative allocation of the meanings 'body' and 'blood' to bread and wine relate to the *distribution* of the elements, to the giving, receiving and consuming of them. The meanings come solely and severely in the context of 'Take, eat' and 'Drink this.' So it is a slightly indirect and even unbiblical question which asks what significance or effect for the bread and wine prior 'consecration' of them may have independently of reception. If we go back to the analogy with baptism, we find that a 'consecration' of the baptismal water is primarily a prayer terminating in an effect on the candidates—and we have seen a similar prayer in Cranmer's 1552 eucharistic rite. So the question recurs—what significance and/or effect does a consecration, as an act in itself prior to the distribution of the sacramental elements, have or imply?

On any account the bread and wine remain unchanged in their appearance and in their chemical construction. On any account there is an attributed significance of 'body' and 'blood' for the purposes of receiving and consuming. Any division of opinion relates to whether some change in the bread and wine occurs which has one or more of the following effects:

1. In some way there is an objective and lasting change in the nature of the elements, perhaps describable as 'transubstantiation';
2. In some way there becomes a 'presence' of Christ identified with the elements, a 'presence' which is located in time and space with, in, or in association with, the elements, and is often described as 'the real presence';
3. The elements become the 'body' and the 'blood' in such a way that the recipient cannot help but eat Christ's body and drink his blood, irrespective of his or her faith, state of heart, discipleship, or reverence.

At this point it is worth setting out the problems such affirmations set:

1. The original words of Jesus were words of distribution;

2. The original context of the Last Supper was whilst Jesus stood before his disciples fully incarnate; and to assert that he held his own body in his hands vitiates the conditions of the incarnation and might well make the crucifixion the next day appear Docetic (that is, in appearance only)—as it is only if Jesus was fully conforming to the conditions of the incarnation that we can with confidence assert that he truly died on the cross. So did he really mean he was holding what was *literally* his body in his hands?

3. The only place to which we can confidently trace the words 'This is my body / blood' is that Last Supper, as the words stem from Jesus and have ever since been used in imitation and repetition of what he said that night. If that night the words were *not* to be taken absolutely literally—that is, that the bread had not become objectively his body or his flesh—then we really have no other reliable point from which to trace the supposed literal change; and, if we dare not be too literal in relation to the elements used at the Last Supper itself, then we would do well to be cautious about being over-literal in relation to post-Pentecost celebrations of the Lord's Supper.[11]

4. There is a fundamental clash between such a doctrine of 'objective' change and the teaching of John chapter 6. There Jesus very clearly states that to eat his flesh is to have eternal life—there are no 'if's and 'but's. But the belief that the bread has at consecration become in a settled and lasting way that body is to allow that the disqualified may eat of it and thus have eternal life by the mere act of eating. The passage has to be placed alongside the warning in 1 Corinthians 11.29 that 'whoever eats this bread and drinks this cup unworthily is guilty of the body and blood of the Lord.' The Reformers took the point that the 'unworthy' eat the bread and drink the cup to their condemnation but were clear that such people do *not* eat the body and drink the blood of Christ. This found its expression in their formulae in the title and text of Article XXIX of the XXXIX Articles 'Of the wicked which eat not the body of Christ in the use of the Lord's Supper.'

There is perhaps one other word of explanation which we can add to help form a coherent doctrine. It is simply this: that the words 'body' and 'blood' point very

---

11 At the risk of labouring the point, the Pauline account in 1 Cor 11.24–25, the main account of the Lord's Supper within the life of the Christian church as recorded in the New Testament, traces the wording back to what Jesus himself said at the original Last Supper. This means that the 'real presence' school of thought concerned must claim that, whatever the meaning of Jesus' words at the Last Supper, those same words have taken up their determinative (ie literal) meaning *since the ascension*, ie since the departure from this earth of the ordinary physical presence of Christ's body and blood. But this conclusion is speculative and improbable, and is based on no evidence—indeed it would appear that, in such an argument, the conclusion has to be reached first and the seeking whatever wisps of evidence might support it has to be added in afterwards. It is a counsel of despair to acknowledge that the primary evidence does not bear upon that conclusion—but then to stick to the conclusion just the same!

strongly to Jesus' death. Whilst the text 'body broken for you' only appears in poor manuscripts, the text 'blood shed for you' has unexceptionable authority. The phrase 'new covenant in my blood' has strong echoes of Moses sprinkling the Israelites with the blood of newly slain animals, and saying 'this is the blood of the covenant' (Exodus 24.8). The Passover context strongly points to the death of the 'Lamb of God.'[12] The John 6 account, whilst it originates from the parallel with the manna in the desert, also runs on to a death reference '...my flesh for the life of the world' (John 6.51). Furthermore there is a Pauline addition to the narrative of institution, and it is an addition which *does* report the actual usage of the Lord's Supper at the time he writes: 'As often as we eat this bread and drink this cup, we tell out the death of the Lord, until he comes' (1 Cor 11.26). This also strongly suggests that the primary point of reference in the words 'body' and 'blood' is the crucifixion, the atonement. It is even possible (though this is more speculative) that Jesus' very provision of a sacrament composed of two separate elements was to indicate body and blood divided from each other in death. If then his death is in fact the main point of reference in the elements, then celebrations of the Supper from Pentecost onwards would have to relate to Jesus' death in one of two ways:

Either   (a) the elements would be pointing to a past event;
or   (b) they would be 'actualizing' it in the present.

In the case of (a) that which is signified is not literally identifiable with the sign; in the case of (b) it is. But the death of Christ, and his sacrifice of himself on the cross, are strongly characterized in the New Testament as 'once-for-all' (*hapax, ephapax*) in time.[13] If we take this seriously, then, whatever relationship across time the church of any age may have with the crucifixion, it cannot be one in which the cross itself is present with us today by eluding time or by being repeated in time or by being somehow summoned out of the past into the present time. We are thus being moved strongly to the solution (a) above. The only obvious alternative would be that 'body' and 'blood' refer in some way to the contemporary physical body of the ascended Christ, in which case the argument has to avoid the central reference to the death of Christ, and, despite all the interpretative New Testament language, conclude that there is some calling down upon earth—more or less into the bread—of the glorified body of Christ. Whole world denominations have reached conclusions of this sort. The only question is whether the scriptural evidence will justify it. Could this conceivably be what Jesus was intending to teach at the Last Supper?

---

12 Quite apart from obvious resemblances in the meal itself, and the fact that Jesus was crucified at Passover time, there are passing references in the New Testament which suggest he saw his death as fulfilling the Passover typology and taught his disciples so (see Luke 9.31, where the Greek word used is '*exodos*'—surely a word with echoes; 1 Cor 5.7; 1 Peter 1.18–19).

13 Compare Heb 7.27; 9.12, 26, 28; 10.2,10; 1 Pet 3.18, and note the 1662 style of 'by his one oblation of himself once offered.'

At this point it will be helpful to go back to an earlier point and recall that the essence of a sacrament is a dynamic conveying of the grace of God by means of administering an 'outward and visible sign,' a material object, to a recipient. Obviously, there could be an explanation which, through a concept of 'making present' with, in, or 'under,' the elements of bread and wine, then taught that that 'presence' is duly conveyed to the recipients as they receive the outward signs. In the last analysis, at the point of reception, and granted that the elements are at that point designated 'body' and 'blood,' very little will hang upon the definitions of how that designation applies or 'works.' There will be liberty of interpretation and room for some restating. But that still leaves questions about 'consecration,' and in particular about how to describe, evaluate and treat 'consecrated' elements prior to, and independently of, actual distribution and consumption. And at that point the Christian world falls into two totally distinguishable halves. These may be respectively dubbed 'objective localization' and 'receptionism'[14]—in each case referring to where, or in what circumstances, the inward part of the sacrament, the body and blood of Christ which are signified by the outward sign, are to be identified as 'present.' We consider the two in order…

Objective Localization

The years from 500 AD to 1200 AD in the Western Church saw an ever increasing emphasis upon the objective 'out-there' reality of the bread as being in itself the body of Christ. It could still be a matter of dispute in the ninth century, as shown in the famous confrontation between Paschasius and Ratram, a brush of theological arms in which the loser was able to save his skin—and , up to a point, Ratram, for all that he *was* the loser, was able to register his 'spiritual' views of the nature of consecration as a possible opinion within the Catholic Church. His opponent, however, Paschasius, better suited the temper of the times and represented a view that was not only advanced towards a quasi-physical change in elements, but also both illustrated and energized a kind of devotional auction, in which, by sheer competitiveness of language, authors and teachers were precipitating a more extreme statement of an 'objective localization' of the body of Christ as identified with the consecrated bread. It is perhaps not surprising that the last author we know to have questioned these doctrinal statements—that is, Berengar in the eleventh century—was viewed as a heretic on the spot, though not condemned (and Ratram was condemned but retrospectively). The Western Church was sliding towards the point where, in 1215, the use of the word 'transubstantiation' by the Fourth Lateran Council was almost more like the holding of the line against doctrines of even-more-miraculous actual physical change in the elements, than it was itself a going 'over the top,' far in advance of teaching that had gone before.

---

14 'Receptionism' is sometimes dubbed 'dynamic symbolism'—a term which equally concentrates on the climactic action of eating and drinking, but sounds less as though the starting point in the action were the recipients!

Transubstantiation, whether in its original 1215 form, or as expounded later in that century by Aquinas, offered and demanded miracle enough—that, whilst the 'accidents' (or attributes) of the bread remained after consecration, these were mere external appearances. The inward reality, which had previously been 'breadness', was now transformed into the body of Christ, *in such a way that it was no longer bread*. The bread had become the body without remainder. It was indeed a miracle, yet, in some ways an awkward one. For, whereas the concept of a miracle or sign in the New Testament was some change or action which impinged *visibly or tangibly* on the senses of those around—and it was that which made it a *thauma*—here was a miracle above all miracles, but one which was simply asserted, and was subject to no possible tests whatsoever.

It should be noted that in the years from 600 to 1300 a large number of liturgical practices and malpractices marched alongside the devotional auction, and both furthered and reflected it. A key factor was, no doubt, the wafer. Once the West had settled down, by conviction, to the use of unleavened bread, then an element which did not give off crumbs and did not readily go stale, offered exactly the medium that was needed to safeguard a doctrine of objective change in the elements. Its origins were innocent enough (should we not follow Jewish Passover practice with unleavened bread, as at the Last Supper itself?), but its outcome was a highly determined, closely defined, doctrine which took the church far from the New Testament.

The devotional accompaniments of the doctrine both illustrated the auction and furthered it. The people ceased to receive the elements, save once a year at Easter. The cup was completely withdrawn from the laity, leaving it as a specially protected and privileged preserve of the clergy, and increasing the mystique attaching to the whole celebration. The priest went round the communion table to preside with his back to the people; and this meant that they could not see the elements, so, at the crucial point of consecration, the priest elevated each element above his head, so that they could now see—and adore. Without a general communion of the people this point of adoration became the centre and climax of the whole rite. The 'sacrament' had moved from the action of giving, receiving and consuming, to the static 'being' of a wafer, which might or might not be about to be eaten, but was undoubtedly the centre of all reverence and adoration irrespective of whether it was eaten. Because the 'sacrament' was the transubstantiated wafer, it became possible also to talk of the 'reserved sacrament,' the 'exposed sacrament,' and 'devotions before the sacrament.' It also became clear that that which I now call 'objective localization' is indeed a reasonable shorthand title for a category of explanations. As long as devotions of various sorts are paid *towards* the elements, so long does the message emerge that a localization of the body of Christ has occurred and is 'there.' This is borne out by liturgical actions such as lifting and demonstrating the elements to the congregation and saying 'This is the Lamb of God who takes away the sins of the world' or 'Behold the Lamb of God...' The 'This is' or the 'Behold' inevitably spring from and point to a concept of localization in or with the demonstrated elements.[15]

The above paragraph is put in strong terms and illustrates Cranmer's conviction that transubstantiation was the chief ill which had befallen the medieval church.[16] But its thrust remains the same even if the severely scholastic concept of transubstantiation is avoided, but a 'real presence' is still asserted, a 'presence' which on inspection, proves to be in, under, or in association with, the actual bread and wine. Any such concept of 'presence' which is recognized and acknowledged in a more-or-less localized way, and is reckoned to originate in or with the elements from the point of consecration onwards, is open to virtually all the objections registered against transubstantiation save the more technical or metaphysical ones.[17]

This in turn means we need to utter a warning about inclusive statements

---

15 Sometimes this assertion is in terms which parallel or reflect the original incarnation—as, for instance:
> 'Though the lowliest form doth veil thee
> as of old at Bethlehem...'

This terminology (if not this hymn) was sufficiently widespread for Cranmer in his time to dub it 'impanation,' as though the Scriptures had said 'The word was made bread and dwelt among us...'

16 This is a classic Cranmerian way of putting it:
> 'But what availeth it to take away beads, pardons, pilgrimages, and such other like popery, so long as two chief roots remain unpulled up? whereof, so long as they remain, will spring again all the former impediments to the Lord's harvest, and corruption of his flock. The rest is but branches and leaves, the cutting away whereof is but like topping and lopping of a tree, or cutting down of weeds, leaving the body standing and the roots in the ground; but the very body of the tree, or rather the roots of the weeds, is the popish doctrine of transubstantiation, of the real presence of Christ's flesh and blood in the sacrament of the altar (as they call it), and of the sacrifice and oblation of Christ made by the priest, for the salvation of the quick and the dead.' (Thomas Cranmer, *On the Lord's Supper* (Oxford: Parker Society, 1844) p 6).

17 Transubstantiation has in fact become embarrassing to the Church of Rome, because the medieval philosophical basis of it has been discredited. In the Anglican-RC Agreement in 1971 the term only appeared as a footnote which stated:
> 'The word *transubstantiation* is commonly used in the Roman Catholic Church to indicate that God acting in the the eucharist effects a change in the inner reality of the elements. The term should be seen as affirming the *fact* of Christ's presence...In contemporary Roman Catholic theology it is not understood as explaining *how* the change takes place' (ARCIC-1, *The Final Report*, p 14).

Rumour has it that it was an Anglican who asked for some mention of the term, and then drafted it, and the Roman Catholics agreed the drafted footnote in a desultory way, but did so for our sakes, without themselves thinking it was worth mentioning! But even if the philosophy is abandoned, we are still up against the term itself from the Fourth Lateran Council (see the text on p 7 above), and also the following Decree from the Council of Trent:
> '...after the consecration of bread and wine, our Lord Jesus Christ, true God and true man, is truly, really and substantially contained in the august sacrament of the Holy Eucharist under the appearance of those sensible things.' (Decree of the Thirteenth Session)

It is the phrase 'under the appearance of' which tells us the doctrine. The elements have *ceased to be bread and wine*—they only have the 'appearance.' It is probably this which led the revisers of the Thirty-Nine Articles to include in the 1571 version that which had been missing in 1553, that 'transubstantiation...overthroweth the nature of a sacrament.' They were saying that a sacrament has an 'outward and visible sign,' but that transubstantiation denies that the outward and visible is still there, so that, by changing the outward into the inward, it leaves no sacrament for it has now no outward sign! However, the main point being made above still stands if the 'localization' concept is spelled out in different terms, and if the bread and wine are thought to be still present even when the divinized localization has taken place.

which affirm that Christ is 'really present' at the Supper. There is, of course, a need for some breadth of meaning to be built into our understanding, both in order that people who belong to each other in Christ but have different views of the Supper may worship together, and in order that individuals may have the opportunity to rethink their own understanding and move along a spectrum of doctrinal formulation without quickly becoming guilty of formal heresy or denominational disloyalty. Nevertheless, when that has been said, affirmations that the 'real presence' of Christ is to be found or known 'in the Supper' should be handled very carefully. They may be deliberately covering up a division between those who think Christ is (in some way) *in* the elements after consecration and those who are saying that when two or three meet in his name (not least for the Supper) Christ is 'present' in their midst. If so, the affirmations would appear to be rather disingenuously concocted.

This distinction is well brought out in the 'Commentary' which accompanies the Lima Statement:

> 'Many churches believe that by the words of Jesus and by the power of the Holy Spirit, the bread and wine of the eucharist become, in a real though mysterious manner, the body and blood of the risen Christ, ie of the living Christ present in all his fullness. Under the signs of bread and wine, the deepest reality is the total being of Christ...Some other churches, while affirming a real presence of Christ at the eucharist, do not link that presence so definitely with the signs of bread and wine.'[18]

This is very overt and therefore helpful. There is an identification of the crack without any papering over of it, and a clear statement that the 'localization' school is indeed stating that the bread and wine *become* 'the living Christ in all his fullness.' As the meanings of the phrase 'real presence' are so vastly different between two schools of thought, it would probably be much better if we could avoid using it.

'Receptionism'

We return to the major alternative view—that the elements change their *signification* but not their essence. In broad terms that makes the consecration of eucharistic elements comparable to the consecration of a building (as, eg, for the purposes of worship) or the consecration of a man (or woman, come to that) as a bishop. In each case the consecration indicates and initiates a change of use, but not a change of nature. The same is true of the consecration of baptismal waters. Consecration is then a setting apart for a specific (and God-given) purpose, and the elements are 'trans-signified,' but not transubstantiated. 'Trans-signification' actually has some respectable history amongst Roman Catholics, but might nevertheless sound like a minimalizing statement to 'localized presence' devotees.

---

18 In 'Commentary' on Eucharist in *Baptism, Eucharist and Ministry* (WCC, 1982) p 12.

What are we then saying? The bread and wine are still bread and wine. We are still receiving 'these thy creatures.' The outward sign is intact. But the signification—the inner reality 'signified'—is the death of Christ and the benefits conveyed to us thereby. We do not have to juggle questions that suggest localization. The elements 'convey' the reality to the true recipient—just as the conveyancing documents for a property 'convey' the property. There is a true reality, a great benefit, thus conveyed, but there is little point in asking in what sense the property itself is 'present' when a transaction is occurring in a solicitor's office. The ARCIC statement, already quoted, was thus very precise (and wholly acceptable) when its wording ran in terms of effectiveness: 'When his people are gathered at the eucharist...Christ makes effective among us the eternal benefits of his victory' and 'The notion of memorial...ie the making effective in the present of an event in the past.'[19] The wording 'makes/making effective' does not claim that an event in the past is itself made present, but that the efficacy of the past event is conveyed in the present.

In this understanding of the dynamic of the sacrament, the true historical place of the cross of Christ is properly protected and yet is also applied to those present. The issue in one sense is common to all doctrines of grace—how is it that that one brief event, the death of one relatively unknown Jewish prophet, in that one small place at one dot-like point in history can possibly affect us to-day? That paradox is relevant in all questions of God's grace. But in this sacramental case it is complicated both by theories that in some sense the original event of past time is itself made present in the present—or alternatively that the presence of Christ today is so exclusively Christ as he is today, that the crucifixion is virtually irrelevant to the Supper, and the linking of the two in Scripture, liturgy and church history is a large-scale, profound and misleading mistake

To those who hold to one form or another of the localization theory, this 're-ceptionist' explanation may seem weak or even a cop-out. It is important, however, to realize that this is not a latterday weakening of a true historic Anglicanism —it is actually a spelling out of the doctrine of the Articles and *Book of Common Prayer*; indeed, this is classic Anglicanism. But in any case, the over-arching question is whether it is true to Scripture; and that has been fully treated above.

How much weight then should be given to the notion that this is a 'weakening' of the truly Christian doctrine? In reply one has to say that it is always both possible and tempting in many fields of worship and pastoral practice to build a doctrine that overstates a truth and distorts it in the process, but is then defended by a cry that it would be a rationalistic 'weakening' to deny that which has been overstated. Thus, to take an example, one enthusiast may assert that all healing ministries must lead to physical healing, another that all prayer for prosperity must bring earthly rewards, a third that the 'grace of orders' will defend the recipient from recurrent temptations or actual sin. These would each be denied, at least in the sweeping form in which they stand, by many truly supernaturalist

---

19 *The Final Report*, pp 12 and 14.

Christian believers on scriptural grounds; and those denials mean that in some sense each is being 'weakened' when it becomes subject to a more nuanced or qualified presentation. However, as I hope the illustration shows, the issue is not how to get into a slightly obsessive auction that is so carried along by its inherent momentum that it outbids both Scripture, true value and common sense; the issue is what statement of the nature of the sacrament is true to Scripture and coherent with other truths. That kind of evaluation need not be 'rationalistic,' but at the same time is proof against the seductiveness of the auction.

Furthermore, there is a fully supernaturalist element yet to be discerned in the account of the Supper given above. Even whilst we work at the meaning of 'body' and 'blood' (and inevitably, for all questions of the effects of consecration concentrate on those words), there is another *motif* interwoven with that meaning. It is tied less obviously to questions of consecration, but it underlies all expositions of the rite. It is simply that we do believe in the presence of Christ with his people; we do believe in his presence when they gather at his table; and we do believe that to be fed by him is to be nourished by his love and bonded to his risen person. There is a wealth of Scripture confirming that view. It is worth reflecting on the following:

a) The meals of Jesus with his disciples in his earthly ministry, particularly the feeding of the five thousand which has strong eucharistic overtones in its terminology (and in the discourse on it in John 6), which were basically meals under Jesus' presidency, in which he gave food to them.[20]

b) The Last Supper itself, the archetype for all interpretation, in which Jesus himself gave them food, but his presence was not literally in the food, but in the person giving the food. Thus he was present to them as the one who loved them, was telling them he was to die for them, and was commissioning them to lives of loving discipleship.

c) The report the two who had gone to Emmaus gave to the eleven when they returned to Jerusalem; for they reported 'how he had been recognized by them in the breaking of the bread' (Luke 24.35). This, as recorded by Luke for his readers thirty or more years later, *must*, surely, have been read with strong sacramental understanding? If the 'breaking of the bread' was a title which meant anything (as Acts 2.42 would suggest it was), then the Emmaus two have to be read as saying that the risen Christ was revealed to them when he acted presidentially at the table.

d) The discourse on the feeding of the five thousand in John 6. Here, whilst there is (as noted on page 10 above) a passage about 'eating the flesh and drinking the blood,' there is also an emphasis upon a simple equation about his person, thus: 'I am the bread of life...I am the living bread. Anyone who eats of this bread will live for ever' (John 6.48,51). An earlier verse has a further equation

---

20 cf also the presidency assumed at Emmaus (Luke 24.30–31), and the meal at the lakeside (John 21.9–13).

in this form: 'Whoever comes to me will never be hungry, and whoever believes in me will never be thirsty' (John 6.35)—and that starts to equate the ingestion of taking food and drink with 'coming' to Jesus and 'believing in Jesus.' And this passage, we must again recall, was being published around 100 AD, with a very clear intention of instructing contemporary believers in the meaning of Communion. It must surely therefore be the living Christ—the ascended Christ who is their contemporary—from whom and on whom they feed.

e) Finally, we need to look at the famous Pauline wording, actually attributed to Jesus himself, that we are to 'do this for remembrance of me' (1 Cor 11.24–25). The 'of me' may not be very strong (it is simply a possessive adjective 'my' in the Greek), but it is clearly of a different order from 'Do this in remembrance of my death.' Had it been in this latter form, then 'remembering' would most obviously be a casting back of the mind to the past event. It would be 'remembering' in the same sense that 'At the going down of the sun and in the morning, we will remember them' is 'remembering.' This latter remembrance does not require us to have known those remembered personally; but it does require us to cast our minds back to the wars and battles in which they perished, and to be grateful for what they achieved. Jesus' command for a 'remembrance of him' is, as I read it, rather different—it is a 'remembrance' of one *who is alive*, who is 'remembered' in his person as we may 'remember' a friend who is at a physical distance, or even 'remember' someone in the same room that we are in. This contrasts strongly with the remembrance of those who died in war, *both* because we know personally the person whom we remember *and* because that person is alive and in varying degrees 'present' with us and to us. It is unnecessary, as well as unfruitful, to create complex concepts of *anamnesis* (remembrance) to make this text somehow the basis for a doctrine of eucharistic sacrifice or of 'actualization' in the present of the death (or other actions of Christ) from the past.

These five considerations point strongly to a doctrine of the living Christ binding us to himself (and thus to each other) by the sacrament in which he, present as the giver at the meal as well as present among his people, mediates afresh to us the benefits and claims of his love. These benefits and claims spring from his death which is central to the message he conveys; he is risen with the power of his redeeming death within him to convey to us; but he does not divide, and we must not divide, between his person and his work. Thus, if we simply are to remember his past death for us, we are open to Dix' complaint of 'a peculiar mental attention to a particular past event.' But, equally, if we are simply to engage with a living deity called 'Jesus Christ,' without reference to his work for us, we are slowly attaching ourselves to an unknown God, a label tied on empty space.

It may be helpful here to add a lesson which I think I originally learned from Roman Catholic authors, notably Nicholas Lash. To be present to a person or at a gathering is not to be defined solely in spatial or juxtapository terms. I may be closely wedged against a dozen others in a tube train, but there is precious little 'I' who am present to those around me. Equally, a letter, a phone-call, an email, or a secret personal gesture in an otherwise anonymous crowd, may make another person intensely present to me. It is only in the knowing of persons as persons that 'being present' has much force—otherwise physical juxtaposition is misdescribed as 'presence.'

It is easy to see how this doctrine can itself be misrepresented. Receptionism has been frequently lampooned as meaning that our faith somehow creates, or at least facilitates, the Lord's presence. The question lingers: is there in fact any truly objective 'given' content to the sacrament at all? Here the ARCIC statement may help again:

> 'In the whole action of the eucharist…the crucified and risen Lord, according to his promise, offers himself to his people…The sacramental body and blood of the Saviour are present as an offering to the believer awaiting his welcome…'[21]

Whilst the word 'offer' may not do full justice to the objectivity we are seeking to describe, it does imply a true 'given,' an objective reality 'there' to be 'offered'; and it also implies that not all who receive the bread and wine will automatically and necessarily receive what is inwardly offered—an exact statement that the outward sign can be received whilst the inward gift signified is (through unbelief or hardness of heart) refused. The outward and inward are, in principle, separable, and John 6.53 (which particularly emphasizes the inward) and 1 Cor 11.29 (which particularly emphasizes the outward) can be read in conjunction with each other without either one violating the force of the other. The title of Article XXIX ('Of the wicked which eat not the body of Christ in the use of the Lord's Supper') is similarly vindicated, as is the thrust of its text.

We are not, however, to end on the harshly logical note of the Reformation test case: what do the wicked receive? We are to find the 'objective' not in the sheerly changed character of the elements independent of reception; instead we are to begin with Christ's salvation, focussed in his vicarious death for us, mediated to us by his risen, living, present person, signified and truly reconveyed to us in and by the eating and drinking of the elements, and bonding us to him and each other anew as the cyclic celebration seizes our lives with his love. And this is not all comfort and relief—'If the sacrament is to communicate to us afresh the benefits of Christ's passion, then we must reaffirm quickly that it also communicates to us the demands of it…If God's grace in the sacrament is as much God re-apprehending us for his service as it is God conveying comfort and relief, then the sacrifice of ourselves…is contemporaneous with the reception…'[22]

---

21 *The Final Report*, pp 13 and 15.
22 COB et al. *Growing into Union: Proposals for Forming a United Church in England* (SPCK, 1970) pp 59–60.

3
What Effects Consecration?

We come now to the other question: what effects consecration? I have suggested above that there is a real case for a 'consecration' preceding the distribution of the elements; and we may strengthen the point for, if we take Jesus' words seriously, then there is a liturgical case for a 'giving thanks' which precedes that distribution. Whilst the assimilation of those two points to each other cannot be totally proved, it looks as though the right thanksgiving (or 'eucharistic') backdrop to the distribution would provide exactly that context within which we could safely identify the elements with the body and blood of Christ, and thus deem them 'consecrated.' However, down history in the West there has been an ever-growing emphasis upon the role of the 'narrative of institution' (hereafter called 'the Narrative') in effecting the consecration. We have seen some early roots of this; and we do find that the liturgical texts from East and West almost invariably include a narrative, quite often as a relative clause ('...who, in the night before he suffered, took bread...'). This might be viewed as a desirable way of pegging our celebration to Jesus' command.[23] But historically it has attracted to itself in the West the concept of providing the actual moment of consecration. So we do well to start with its role.

The Narrative of Institution
Clearly the Narrative can be read as simply a warrant before any action begins. It has developed that way in some non-episcopal circles, and even in congregations used to extemporary worship it may well provide a scriptural or quasi-scriptural text on the basis of which the sacramental meal and its particular manner of celebration can then be conducted. However, there has often been a parallel development, one to which Lutherans, to take but one example, have often subscribed. It is the use of the Narrative, in a way that looks as free-standing as the 'warrant' usage, but using it as itself *being* the action, so that the elements are viewed as consecrated (or 'set apart,' as many would say) by the sheer recitation of the Narrative so that all that remains to be done is the distribution.

From a liturgical point of view, the 'warrant' use is extremely interesting, and, although it has no Patristic roots, it offers a satisfying way of developing a four-action shape from a clear starting-point. The difficulty lies in the other school of thought, for there are very large numbers of Christians who apparently cannot divorce from their minds the concept of the Narrative as consecratory. These peo-

---

23 To take one instance, the Church of North India, which in the 1980s produced a rite not unlike Rite A, also allowed the Narrative to be taken out of the eucharistic prayer and cited as a warrant text before the action began. A very good and pioneering unofficial attempt on these lines was made in England in the seminal *Eucharist for the Seventies*, edited by Trevor Lloyd and Christopher Byworth in 1968 and published by the press which became Grove Books.

ple are deeply schooled by Western history into thinking that the repetition of Jesus' own words consecrates, and thus, irrespective of the context of the Narrative in the rite, resist attempts to use it in a way which clearly does not consecrate.

What then is this history? The general view of Western authors from early times seems to have been that the words of institution ('This is my body' and 'This is my blood') during the Narrative of institution actually effected the change. The discussion always saw the Narrative not in a free-standing way as above, but within the eucharistic prayer, the thanksgiving. However, the locating of consecration in the dominical words was systematized and set out starkly in the twelfth century by Peter Lombard who, in his *Sententiae*, provided the whole pattern of 'seven sacraments' which has been dominant in the Roman Catholic Church since. About consecration he wrote as follows:

> '[Christ's words effect the change] saying "This is my body" and afterwards "This is my blood." For when these words are uttered, then takes place the change of the bread and wine into the substance of the Body and Blood of Christ: the rest is said to the praise of God.'[24]

So here is a clear doctrine. We now know the moment of the change—at least in Lombard's view. And, if we follow his argument aright, he is somewhat unworried by the context—the Narrative could even be free-standing, for all the weight he gives to the rest of the eucharistic prayer. Yet, curiously, the Fourth Lateran Council in 1215, whilst picking up the 'substance' terminology and imposing transubstantiation, did *not* define what brings about the change. The same was true later of the Council of Trent, so that, although it appears that the standard, widely believed, Roman doctrine is that the words of institution effect consecration, it is not *de fide*, and can even be rethought.[25] To an outside onlooker, this is absolutely staggering—that the most mind-blowing miracle occurs within the liturgy and must be affirmed and recognized as occurring, yet, within a Church which in all other respects gives definitive answers to mysteries, there is actually no certainty as to the conditions under which that miracle occurs.

Although there is a tremendously strong tradition of ceremonial accompaniments to the Narrative, and a widespread use of large capitals for the dominical words in the printings of the rite, neither of these strong hints actually achieves *de fide* or infallible status.

Part of the problem in the Roman Catholic position is that, since the Great

---

24 Lombard, *Sententiae* 4.8.4

25 I write this with first-hand experience of Roman Catholics who have been prepared to question it, and to point out it was not in fact *de fide*. Indeed, years ago I started a correspondence with Mgr J D Crichton about just this point, assuming the matter had been infallibly defined somewhere (perhaps at the Fourth Lateran Council), and urging that the very printing of the page in liturgical books (where the dominical words often appear in large capitals or otherwise highlighted) was strong evidence of Roman dogma. He courteously replied to me that my case was, from the point of view of Roman Catholic history, not proven. I reopened the correspondence when writing this booklet, and he now confirms that such a moment not only has not been defined, but actually could not be because of the Eastern rites which I discuss below.

Schism in 1054 between Rome and the Eastern Orthodox Churches, Rome has itself fostered 'Uniat' Churches, ie Churches which use Eastern rites, but are under the aegis of Rome. Eastern eucharistic prayers appear strongly to focus as the point and agent of consecration the epiclesis (or calling upon the Father to send the Spirit onto or into the elements to 'make' them the body and blood of Christ)—and the epiclesis comes in the Eastern rites *after* the Narrative. It is thus extremely difficult to sustain in those rites the notion that the words of institution effect the consecration. The Church of Rome, on the strictest view, asserts that consecration effects transubstantiation, but is *not* wholly clear as to what effects consecration. And it is difficult to believe that God changes his mind—or is simply at our disposal—according to which rite we choose to use.

What then of the Church of England—and of worldwide Anglicanism? We have seen that the eucharistic rite in Cranmer's second *Prayer Book* had no point of consecration other than in the distribution and reception of the elements. However, in Elizabeth I's reign, with the same book in use, it became conventional to insist that the Narrative, still prominently there in the rite, *was* the consecration. This rationale persisted, and led in the 1604 Canons to a requirement for a repetition of the Narrative if supplementary consecration were ever needed. Later, in 1662, the rationale was set in concrete by a series of small further changes round Cranmer's text:

a) Rubrics referred to preparing the table and putting the elements on it (previously they were not mentioned until the distribution!);
b) The 'sacramental prayer' (it had no title in 1552) was now 'The Prayer of Consecration';
c) Five indented rubrics providing for five 'manual acts' were inserted beside the Narrative (previously, as there had been no rubrical mention of the elements, there had been equally no requirement to 'manipulate' them);
d) The prayer was closed by an 'Amen';
e) After the distribution, provision was made for supplementary consecration by repetition of the relevant part of the Narrative;
f) After the end of the service, a requirement was made that all 'consecrated remains' should be consumed (previously there had by definition been no 'consecrated' remains and so any bread and wine outstanding went home with the curate *'for his own use'*).

1662 thus tightly prescribed that consecration was effected by the Narrative, a practice which Frere once called 'more Roman than Rome.' But the question of what effects consecration remains a different question from what consecration effects; and Frere's dictum, whilst it accurately described an identity of practice as to what effected consecration, had no bearing whatsoever on the other question, as to whether we had any resemblance to Roman doctrine in our understanding of what consecration effected.

The Eastern Epiclesis

The Eastern rites, from the earliest traceable texts to the present time, have had a full-blown epiclesis at a later point in the prayer than the Narrative (usually in fact after an anamnesis, itself following the Narrative). This (as we have seen) is hardly compatible with the Lombard doctrine of consecration, and inevitably sets the Narrative aside as *not* effecting consecration. Yet Rome has given full recognition to the propriety of Eastern (or Uniat) churches within the Roman fold, and their Eastern-style rites are fully accepted in Rome.

A regular cycle of waves of enthusiasm for Eastern-style epicleses can be found in Anglicanism. It starts with the Scottish Episcopal rite of 1764 in this form:

'And we most humbly beseech thee, O merciful Father, to hear us, and of thy almighty goodness vouchsafe to bless and sanctify, with thy word and Holy Spirit, these thy gifts and creatures of bread and wine, that, being blessed and hallowed by his life-giving power, they may become the Body and Blood of thy most dearly beloved Son.'

Here, it may be noted, there is not only a problem about the position of such an epiclesis in the eucharistic prayer, but also a problem about the content of the prayer, as the work of the Spirit thus invoked appears to terminate not on the eucharistic action or the recipients, but rather upon the elements in themselves.

Thus a variant on the Scottish text was then found in America, where the colonies were much 'lower' in their churchmanship. After Seabury's consecration by the Scottish bishops in 1784, he returned to Connecticut with a *concordat* and a copy of their eucharist, but was unable to persuade the General Convention of 1789 to sail as near to Scotland as he would have wished. The result was an epiclesis of a much more obviously 'receptionist' kind:

'And we most humbly beseech thee, O merciful Father, to hear us, and, of thy almighty goodness, vouchsafe to bless and sanctify, with thy Word and Holy Spirit, these thy gifts and creatures of bread and wine, that we, receiving them according to thy Son our Saviour Jesus Christ's holy institution, in remembrance of his death and passion, may be partakers of his most blessed Body and Blood.'

Here there is an interesting combination of thoughts, clearly based on the Scottish text, but equally clearly deliberately amended in a 'receptionist' direction. The crucial continuity, however, is that this epiclesis still follows the Narrative, and thus virtually precludes the Narrative from being itself the point of consecration. The Eastern pattern has had an intermittent innings in Anglicanism, being favoured not only in the eighteenth century, but also in the first half of the twentieth (as, for example, in the 1928 Book, where the Roman-facing Anglo-catholics could not be induced to use it)—and now very recently in the forms of eucharistic prayer proposed by the Liturgical Commission, without a vast amount of compelling theological reasoning, but with the anodyne (or meretricious?) title 'the Trinitarian shape.'[26] The most recent also include at one point, prior to revision, that which has never previously been authorized in the Church of England (but can be seen elsewhere in the Anglican Communion, deriving from the Scottish model above), a calling of the Holy Spirit *into* or *onto* the elements.[27]

The petition for consecration which, in Western-pattern prayers, often *precedes* the Narrative, is wholly compatible with a doctrine which locates consecration in the dominical words in the Narrative, and thus hardly affects the argument above. It may or may not include mention of the Spirit, but it is regularly called the 'epiclesis.' Clearly Lombard did not view it as ultimately necessary; and we, whilst valuing a petition that looks forward to a total pattern of consecration, do not have to see it as necessary either—and a petition for the fruitfulness of the action may well come at a later stage in the rite. The present Liturgical Commission is not above suspicion of having a motive of weaning Anglicans from centring too heavily upon the Narrative by abolishing the 'Western' style 'first epiclesis,' and putting all the weight of consecration into a later epiclesis in the Eastern position. If this suspicion is true, it has this much credibility—that the eucharistic prayers in Rite A, which have the Western 'first epiclesis' before the Narrative (and in the case of the Third Prayer have a visible origin in Rome[28]), are regularly used with farced ceremonial in the Narrative as though they had been composed purely on Lombard's principles. But such was not the case, and maybe weaning is needed.

Thanksgiving as Consecration

We come to the emerging way through. There has been an ever-increasing mood in the twentieth century to see the whole of the eucharistic prayer—the thanksgiving—as consecratory.[29] This is in line with the sense that we are follow-

---

26 The outworking of this 'shape' is that the Preface relates to God the Father, the Narrative and anamnesis to God the Son, and the epiclesis (and petitions for fruitful reception) to God the Holy Spirit. It is vigorously written up in a keynote essay by the American Episcopalian, Thomas Talley, in the 'Untermarchtal' papers—David Holeton (ed), *Revising the Eucharist* (Alcuin/GROW Joint Liturgical Study No 27, Cambridge: Grove Books, 1994). The clutch of new prayers written on this basis, which occupied the Church of England in the mid-1990s, can be seen in the collection of rejected texts, COB and Trevor Lloyd (ed), *Six Eucharistic Prayers as Proposed in 1996* (Grove Worship Series No 136, 1996).

27 Prayer E in the new batch of six which went through General Synod in July 1998 contains such a petition. Some of the prayers which ended up as the rejected six in 1996 had started life similarly, but the particular Revision Committee insisted on changing the text of each to ensure that the Spirit was invoked on the action, not the elements.

28 The prayer was submitted to the Revision Committee by Brian Brindley and Roger Beckwith in 1978 in a form which was nearer to the Roman Prayer II, based on Hippolytus, than it now has—for the Revision Committee worked hard over it. For a comparison of texts by folding charts see COB (ed), *The New Eucharistic Prayers of the Church of England* (Grove Liturgical Study No 20, 1979) or *Latest Anglican Liturgies 1976–84* (Alcuin/SPCK, 1985). Hippolytus himself of course did not have a Western epiclesis, but Rome had inserted it, and Rite A provided one in accord with the other eucharistic prayers in the rite.

29 It appears that, as far back as 1924, the South African bishops had defended their experimental rite (with an Eastern type of epiclesis) as based on the concept that consecration is effected by thanksgiving, which was taken up and issued almost as a novelty in the 1958 Lambeth Conference report. But those older texts kept many of the more 'Roman' features of 1662 even whilst making this proclamation.

ing Jesus' command in 'giving thanks,' and that doing that part of his given order aright is the appropriate reassurance for going on to the next part of his order, for it is within that context that we shall be fully able to say 'This is the Lord's Supper, and within it we shall receive this bread and this cup as feeding us on the body and blood of Christ.' From a scriptural point of view this is a far higher doctrine than the quasi-magical Lombard one—which downgrades praise and thanksgiving as mere adjuncts instead of making them as a whole integral to the action.[30] The difficulty is that, if a Narrative (even in an adjectival clause) appears, as is always likely to be the case, the traditional 'Western' orientated persons are liable to build their devotional and ceremonial accoutrements around the Narrative as if it alone were consecratory. Similarly, any petition for fruitful reception, however innocent, is liable at least to be tested and sifted to see if it is a true epiclesis or not, though straight 'Eastern' views of consecration are not so prevalent as 'Western' ones. And it has to be confessed that a broad view of the consecratory character of the whole prayer is easier for those who believe that consecration effects a change of use and signification than it is for those who hold that somehow the nature, the substance or the ontology is being changed. In the light of this it is interesting that ARCIC-1 could write:

> 'Before the eucharistic prayer, to the question: "What is that?", the believer answers: "It is bread." After the eucharistic prayer, to the same question he answers: "It is truly the body of Christ, the Bread of Life."'[31]

The ways by which the Liturgical Commission in the years 1965–80 got away from a special moment of consecration to a more 'scene-setting' concept can be traced in the texts. In Series 2 Communion in 1967 the Commission was forced to accept two manual acts within the Narrative, which half-suggested a Roman doctrine (at least of 'what effects…'). In Series 3 Communion in 1971 the Commission had a rubric 'The President takes the bread and wine' under a cross-heading of 'The Taking of the Bread and Wine' prior to the eucharistic prayer—and no mention of manual acts within the eucharistic prayer itself at all. Thus the 'taking' could in no sense be identified with a moment of consecration, and the eucharistic prayer became more like a single seamless backdrop to the later distribution, defining it and enabling the rite to be identified as the Lord's Supper, but without highlighting or weighting any one paragraph. The Narrative then took its rightful grammatical place as a dependent clause within a larger set of thought-forms.

In Rite A in the *ASB* further steps were taken to build up this understanding. In the opening Notes it was stated that the prayer is a single prayer throughout

---

30 Is there ancient precedent apart from the original Narrative passages of Scripture? Well, Justin Martyr certainly writes of the elements being 'eucharisticized' into the body and blood of Christ, and tells us of the president offering up thanksgiving at exactly the point where we now have our 'eucharistic' prayer (introduced by 'Let us *give thanks* to the Lord our God.'

31 'Elucidation' of the Statement on the Eucharist, para 6, *The Final Report*, p 21. My interest in it at this point is solely in relation to how it sees what effects consecration.

and changes of posture during it are unhelpful (p 115). And in the structuring of the rite a changed cross-heading read 'The Taking of the Bread and the Cup and the Giving of Thanks.' There then followed the rubric, designed to help give a clean four-action shape to the sacramental rite, *'The president takes the bread and cup into his hands and replaces them on the holy table.'*

Exactly this point was made by the International Anglican Liturgical Consultation at Dublin in 1995. This Consultation (known as IALC-5), with liturgists from over half the provinces of the Anglican Communion, unanimously found as follows:

'The fundamental character of the eucharistic prayer is thanksgiving, and the whole eucharistic prayer should be seen as consecratory. The elements of memorial and invocation are caught up within the movement of thanksgiving.'[32]

Once that point has been gathered, then, as the Dublin findings indicate, the exact relationship to each other of the Narrative and epicletic material may not matter so much. The ethos has moved far from the notion of a 'moment' of consecration (for all the persistence of those ceremonial accoutrements). What we need if we are to continue the concept of consecration is a vivid verbal backdrop, put in 'eucharistic' terms, with some reference back to the Lord's command in order to make clear our purpose. If, we might mischievously add, that purpose will be most clearly identified, then we could well return to the point where this chapter started—a preliminary reading of the Narrative as a 'warrant' text, followed by a discrete 'taking' and a full thanksgiving without the Narrative in it.[32]

---

32 See David R Holeton (ed) *The Renewal of the Anglican Eucharist* (Grove Worship Series No 135) and David R Holeton (ed) *Our Thanks and Praise: the Eucharist in Anglicanism Today—Papers from the Fifth International Anglican Liturgical Consultation* (ABC, Toronto, 1998) p 262.

33 The situation is complicated by various other accretions prior to the sacramental action. This is particularly true of the Roman (so-called) 'offertory prayers.' Quite apart from any problem they cause by their emphasis on 'offering' the elements to God, or from simply holding up the action, they also threaten the basic order and the rationale of the eucharistic prayer by providing thanksgivings over bread and cup such as virtually to conform to the requirements for the eucharistic prayer itself, and I occasionally meet discerning 'high' church people who have scruples about whether the elements have not been consecrated too early, by the use of such ambiguous prayers! Within the original ARCIC-1 statement we learn 'Christ's body and blood become really present and are really given,' and the word 'become' has suggested an objective change; yet the statement is not only reticent, as we have seen, about what consecration effects (viz transubstantiation) but is also slightly elusive on what effects consecration. Its text at this point reads '...the consecratory prayer (anaphora) leads to the communion of the faithful. Through this prayer of thanksgiving, a word of faith addressed to the Father, the bread and wine become the body and blood of Christ...' (*The Final Report*).

4
Appendix: Loose Ends

I offer some consequential reflections upon two of the phenomena which have arisen amongst Anglicans, through the weight placed by the 1662 *Book of Common Prayer* upon the concept of consecration and the role of the Narrative in effecting it.

Supplementary Consecration

1552, which had no consecration separate from distribution and reception, inevitably had no provision for supplementary consecration if the supply ran out. Presumably the minister simply got more of either element and went on distributing. However, in Elizabeth's reign, it became a matter of policy to insist that there is an objective consecration in the 1552 rite—and thus supplementary supplies came by repeating the Narrative, or the necessary part of it. This extra-rubrical requirement was in due course enshrined in the 1604 Canons, and in 1662 inserted into the *BCP* rubrics. As 1662 locates consecration in the Narrative (with a touching of every vessel holding bread or wine to be consecrated), supplementary consecration is done by repetition and corresponding designation.

Repetition has generally held the field where the Narrative or an epiclesis have been held to be consecratory (though it is difficult when it includes both!). But the concept of repetition has itself come under question with the modern rites; and it is very frequently heard that, if the original eucharistic prayer offers a context, then supplementation ought to be done by extending the context to include new supplies. The obvious parallel is at a dinner with guests, where, though the 'president' of the meal may initially give God thanks, no-one would expect those thanks to be repeated if more food is brought from the kitchen. On the other hand, the logic of taking more unobtrusively and/or in silence has seemed over-frightening to people who still have a notion of repetition. The result so far has been the provision of unsatisfactory, though not quite repetitive, texts for reading aloud.[34] But, if the argument in chapter 3 about the eucharistic prayer as setting a

---

[34] The historical oddity here is that, in the original Series 3 communion in 1971, the Commission took the advice of the Doctrine Commission that silence would do perfectly well. Lovers of the 'moment of consecration' appealed in General Synod to the then Archbishop of Canterbury, Michael Ramsey, to state his view. He said that he shuddered with all his being from the thought that the greatest thing that ever happens on earth—ie the consecration of bread and wine—should happen without anyone present even knowing it was happening. The Synod promptly eliminated the permission to take more in silence. But 26 years experience in many contexts since then have made it clear to me that no-one really expects the congregation to know, that muttering over one or other element in a corner whilst others proceed with a distribution is very regular, and that, even when I am presiding, I may turn round to find some assisting presbyter has taken it upon himself or herself to do that muttering without my knowledge. I believe Michael Ramsey's criterion to be entirely irrelevant and misleading.

context be taken seriously, then bringing more bread and wine into the context should be viewed as consecratory.

If designation is to be done more exactly, then any of the following would help that designation:

(a) further supplies should be added to existing supplies *before* the stock is exhausted;

(b) any adding of more should be done exclusively by the president;

(c) any adding of more should be done on the central communion table.

With these provisos, then adding in silence ought to be permitted.

What is wholly clear is that, once the point is taken that consecration is by the use of the whole eucharistic prayer, then supplementary consecration by the repetition of some short formula is not a possible option—the question *has* to be how to take the eucharistic context as given, and then bring more of one or other element into the rite as consecrated by that rite.

Reservation

Whilst 1662 provided a clear concept of consecration in and through the dominical words in the Narrative, it also took steps to ensure that there could be no superstitious treatment of consecrated elements—for any remaining at the end of the distribution were to be reverently consumed. This was in clear contrast to the developed Roman pattern of reserving consecrated wafers and using those reserved elements for devotional purposes—perhaps an entirely logical development in a Church which believed its wafers were being transubstantiated.

The provision for consumption actually guarded the Church of England's clergy against accusations of both irreverence and superstition. It has been an oddity of the last hundred years that reservation of consecrated elements—and devotions towards them and with them—has flourished and been encouraged (however 'superstitious'), whilst any hint anywhere that consecrated elements have been disposed of otherwise than by reverent consumption has tended to raise a storm. It was not, however, the 'irreverent' who so flagrantly breached the terms of the 1662 settlement. There is a vast history of the debates of the twentieth century on the issue of reservation—suffice to say here that nothing exposes two widely sundered understandings of 'what consecration effects' more than the partisan zeal for reservation, and for the cultus of the reserved elements.[35] This is not, of course, in any way to discountenance the taking of consecrated elements to the sick and shut-ins in order that they may share in an 'extended' way in the main celebration of a parish.

---

35 There has been a twist in relation to the cultus, in that the Pope thought he had been given insufficient guarantees, in the ARCIC-1 treatment of the eucharist, of the Anglican commitment to the cultus, and so he asked for more—and ARCIC-2 wrote *Clarifications* especially to meet his concern, and in the course of it quoted the 1662 rubric about consuming the remains as evidence of the high reverence we have for the consecrated elements, from which the Pope can see our readiness for devotions to or before the reserved elements! There seemed some dog-leg logic to it, that ARCIC should demonstrate our love of reservation from our rubric requiring consumption.